T0283467

Power of the Written Goal

- by Jason Cardiff

Table of Contents

Topics

About the Author

From the very outset of his entrepreneurial journey, Jason Cardiff has epitomized the spirit of success at all costs. Driven by an unwavering determination and an unquenchable thirst for innovation, Jason's relentless pursuit of his goals has consistently placed him at the forefront of diverse industries. His journey is a testament to his embodiment of the principle that achieving success often demands the willingness to make sacrifices, overcome challenges, and push boundaries.

Jason's path to success has been marked by a consistent willingness to confront challenges head-on. Whether it was overcoming regulatory hurdles, defending against legal battles, or navigating the complexities of emerging industries, his tenacity and resilience have remained unwavering. These challenges, far from deterring him, have only fueled his drive to prove that success can be attained, even in the most demanding circumstances.

The pursuit of success at all costs requires a willingness to break new ground and pioneer unexplored territories. Jason's portfolio of ventures, from media and marketing to thin film technologies, electronic cigarettes, and medical supplies, reflects his ability to identify opportunities beyond conventional boundaries. His commitment to exploring new avenues demonstrates his unwavering belief that success lies where others fear to tread.

Success at all costs often necessitates personal sacrifice and unrelenting dedication. Jason's journey exemplifies his willingness to make these sacrifices in order to achieve his vision. His track record of building and leading multiple successful companies demonstrates his capability to achieve significant milestones while staying true to his relentless pursuit of progress.

Jason Cardiff's commitment to success at all costs extends beyond individual ventures—it is a philosophy that has permeated every facet of his life. His dedication to excellence, as evidenced by his thriving businesses and his role as a loving husband and father, reflects his belief that success is not confined to one area but is a way of life.

In a world that often demands compromise, Jason Cardiff stands as a beacon of inspiration for those who aspire to achieve greatness on their own terms. His unwavering commitment to pushing boundaries, confronting challenges, and maintaining a relentless pursuit of success serves as a reminder that the journey to success is not always smooth, but it is the unwavering pursuit that defines a true success-at-all-costs champion.

Jason Cardiff's journey is a testament to his embodiment of the philosophy of success at all costs. His trailblazing endeavors, his resilience in the face of challenges, and his commitment to achieving excellence have left an indelible mark on various industries. Through his unwavering pursuit of success, he demonstrates that achieving greatness requires embracing risks, overcoming obstacles, and steadfastly adhering to a vision, regardless of the challenges encountered along the way.

Famous Quotes to Get You Started

Success often speaks through the mouths of those, who have already achieved it. This is why, I wanted to begin this book with some of the most popular and inspiring quotes that have always helped me keep striving to be the best version of myself. So, if you had any doubts about how written goals can help make you more successful, here are quotes by some famous people to inspire you and prepare you for the learning that is about to come:

1.   "Imagination is the compass; a written goal is the map. Together, they chart the course to brilliance." - Albert Einstein

2.   "Words are our stepping stones to destiny. Write your goals with purpose and watch your path unfold." - Maya Angelou

3.   "Innovation begins with intention. Put your goals in writing, and you've already taken the first step toward changing the world." - Steve

Jobs

4.   "A written goal is a declaration to the universe. It says, 'I will not be limited by my circumstances; I will shape them." - Nelson Mandela

5.   "Your life is your story, and your goals are its chapters. Write them down with conviction, and watch as your narrative transforms." - Oprah
Winfrey

6.   "Dreams become tangible when you put them on paper. The ink becomes the blueprint for the magic that follows." - Walt Disney

7.   "Words have the power to change history. So, write your goals as if the world is waiting for your story." - Abraham Lincoln

8.   "In the tapestry of life, written goals are the threads that weave our desires into reality." - Jane Austen

9.   "The spark of an idea can light up the world, but a written goal ignites the path toward its realization." - Thomas Edison

10.   "The future belongs to those who believe in the beauty of their written goals." - Eleanor Roosevelt

11.   "Written goals are the bridges between our dreams and the journey we must take to reach them." - Martin Luther King Jr.

12.   "As a canvas holds the artist's vision, so does paper hold the dreams of the visionary. Write your goals and paint your life." - Leonardo da Vinci

Introduction

The roadmap to wholesome success is not easy! You need to unleash your full potential to be the best version of yourself in every walk of your life. My life has been a series of hit and trial, and after I cracked the right ways to go about it, I thought it to be only wise to share my insights with others in need. One of my key success mantras is writing down your desirable goals, and I firmly believe that starting off with some famous quotes on the same line.

You must be curious about how penning down what you want helps achieve it. Hence, I wrote this book to help you embrace the transformative power of setting written goals, so that you can embark on the never-ending journey to success. Not only will this book provide practical strategies for achieving success across all facets of life, but it will also help set the tone for personal growth and accomplishment. I sincerely hope that you enjoy your read and find it worthy enough to be recommended to others around you.

With much love!
- Jason Cardiff

Chapter 1: Goal Setting and Imagination

Let's start the first and one of the most important chapters of the book by unveiling the connection between imagination, goals and success. If you are wondering about the use of imagination in this thoughtful endeavor, let me try to be clearer with the rule of thumb that has always keep me going - 'Imagination is your compass; written goals are your roadmap. Together, they lead you to the extraordinary life you envision.'

And so, the journey of starting to live your dream life begins by crafting powerful goals by learning some techniques to tap into your creative imagination. You need to understand that in the pursuit of success in every area of your life, the first step is to harness the remarkable power of your imagination and channel it through the art of goal setting. Your imagination is the wellspring of creativity and innovation; it's the force that propels dreams into reality. When coupled with the structured guidance of written goals, your imagination becomes a driving force that shapes your journey to success.

Imagination, often associated with creativity and fantasy, is a powerful cognitive ability that plays a significant role in setting life goals. It is the mental canvas upon which we paint our dreams and aspirations, the catalyst that propels us to envision a future beyond our current reality. While some might perceive imagination as a flight of fancy, it is, in fact, a fundamental element in the process of goal-setting. In this part of the book, let us explore why imagination is crucial in setting life goals, and examine its role in fostering motivation, innovation, adaptability, and personal growth.

At its core, setting life goals is an act of envisioning the desired future. Imagination serves as the ignition to this process of fueling motivation and determination. Without the ability to imagine a better tomorrow, individuals may find themselves stuck in the inertia of the present, lacking the drive to pursue meaningful goals.

Imagination allows us to create vivid mental pictures of our desired outcomes, providing a source of inspiration and emotional connection to our objectives. These mental images act as beacons guiding our actions and choices. For instance, someone dreaming of becoming a successful entrepreneur envisions the day their innovative product changes the world. This mental image serves as a constant source of motivation, pushing them through the inevitable challenges of entrepreneurship.

Furthermore, imagination can help individuals visualize the benefits and rewards of achieving their goals. This visualization generates a sense of anticipation and excitement, making the pursuit of those goals more enticing. It transforms abstract goals into tangible, emotionally charged objectives that one is willing to work tirelessly to achieve.

Innovation is the cornerstone of progress, and imagination is the precursor to innovation. In the pursuit of life goals, individuals often encounter obstacles and roadblocks that require creative solutions. Imagination serves as the wellspring from which these innovative ideas flow.

Consider the field of technology. Innovations like smartphones, electric cars and social media platforms were once mere figments of someone's imagination. Visionaries like Steve Jobs, Elon Musk, and Mark Zuckerberg harnessed their creative imagination to envision products and solutions that revolutionized industries.

The role of imagination in innovation extends beyond technology. It's evident in fields such as Art, Science and Literature. Visionaries like Leonardo da Vinci and Albert Einstein imagined possibilities that expanded the boundaries of their respective disciplines. They utilized their imagination to formulate groundbreaking theories and create works of art that continue to inspire and shape our world even today.

In a personal context, imagination encourages us to think outside the box when confronted with challenges or setbacks in the pursuit of our life goals. It enables us to explore alternative approaches, adapt to changing circumstances, and find creative solutions to obstacles. Imagination, therefore, not only sets the stage for innovation but also equips individuals with the tools to overcome adversity on their journey to achieving their goals.

In the journey of life, unexpected twists and turns are inevitable. The ability to adapt to new circumstances and re-calibrating one's goals is essential for long-term success and fulfillment. Imagination plays a crucial role in fostering this adaptability.

Imagination allows individuals to explore different scenarios and anticipate potential challenges or opportunities. By mentally rehearsing various outcomes, individuals can prepare themselves to pivot when necessary. This flexibility in goal-setting is particularly valuable in an everchanging world where the ability to adapt can make the difference between success and stagnation.

Moreover, when individuals possess a rich imaginative capacity, they are more likely to embrace change as an opportunity rather than a threat. They can envision new possibilities and adapt their goals accordingly, harnessing their creative thinking to transform setbacks into stepping stones.

For example, consider an individual who aspired to become a professional athlete but suffered a career-ending injury. Through the power of imagination, they might envision a new path, perhaps coaching or sports management, which aligns with their passion and skills. Imagination enables them to pivot and pursue a different but equally fulfilling goal.

Setting life goals is not merely about external achievements; it is also a journey of personal growth and self-discovery. Imagination plays a significant role in this aspect by encouraging individuals to explore their values, desires, and identities.

When one engages their imagination to set life goals, they delve deep into their inner world, asking fundamental questions about what truly matters to them. They envision the kind of life they want to lead, the values they want to uphold, and the impact they want to make on the world. This process of introspection and self-reflection is essential for personal growth.

Moreover, as individuals strive to achieve their goals, they often encounter obstacles that require personal development and growth. Imagination, by allowing them to see their potential and envision a better version of themselves, serves as a catalyst for self-improvement.

Consider someone who dreams of becoming a successful author. Along their journey, they may face self-doubt, writer's block and rejection. Imagination can help them visualize their growth as a writer, envisioning themselves mastering the craft, receiving acclaim for their work, and contributing to the literary world. This mental image becomes a powerful motivator for them to persevere, improve their skills, and evolve as a writer.

It will not be wrong to say that imagination plays a pivotal role in setting life goals, serving as a driving force behind motivation, innovation, adaptability and personal growth. It empowers individuals to dream big, envision a brighter future, and take the necessary steps to turn those dreams into reality. Imagination is not a mere flight of fancy; it is the spark that ignites the journey towards meaningful and fulfilling life goals.

As we navigate the complexities of life, it is essential to recognize and nurture our imaginative capacity. By doing so, we can harness the transformative power of imagination to set and achieve goals that not only enhance our own lives but also contribute to the betterment of society as a whole. Imagination is not a luxury; it is an indispensable tool for creating a future that aligns with our deepest aspirations and values.

As we have already discussed, imagination is a remarkable human capability that plays a pivotal role in shaping our lives, our achievements, and our overall well-being. It's the spark that ignites innovation, fuels creativity, and drives progress in every field of human endeavor. Whether you're an entrepreneur striving to launch a groundbreaking startup, an artist seeking to create a masterpiece, or a scientist exploring the frontiers of knowledge, harnessing the power of imagination is crucial for achieving success. Let us understand how to delve deep into the realm of imagination, explore what it is, why it matters, and most importantly, how to cultivate and leverage it for success.

Before we delve into the strategies for cultivating imagination power, it's essential to grasp the concept of imagination and its various facets. So, let us start with the basic question – what really is imagination? Imagination is the mental faculty that allows us to create mental images, concepts, and ideas that are not directly derived from our sensory experiences. It enables us to envision things that are not currently present in our physical reality, whether they are fantasies, possibilities, or innovative solutions to problems.

Imagination is a powerful cognitive process that combines creativity, memory, and the ability to visualize. It is not a monolithic concept, but consists of several components, each serving a unique purpose. Here are the key components of imagination for you to master step-by-step:

Creativity and Visualization: Creativity is the foundation of imagination. It involves generating novel ideas, concepts, and connections between seemingly unrelated elements. Creative thinking is the engine that drives imaginative processes. Visualization is the ability to form mental images. It allows you to see, hear or otherwise experience the products of your imagination in your mind's eye. Visualization is a crucial skill for artists, designers and even problem solvers.

Conceptualization and Empathy: Imagination also involves the ability to form abstract concepts and ideas. This is essential for envisioning and understanding complex systems, theories and paradigms. Empathy allows you to imagine the experiences, thoughts and feelings of others. It plays a great role in various learning processes like creating characters in Literature, understanding different perspectives, and fostering meaningful relationships.

Memory: Memory is closely linked to imagination because it provides the raw material for constructing mental scenarios. Memories of past experiences, knowledge and information serve as building blocks for imagination. Imagination is not just a whimsical trait; it can serve as the fundamental driver of success in various domains.

Now let us discuss some reasons that are compelling enough for you to cultivate your imagination power for achieving success. The first attribute on our list is innovation and problem solving! Imagination is the wellspring of innovation. Successful entrepreneurs, inventors and scientists often credit their ability to envision novel solutions to solve complex problems as a key factor in their success. Imagination helps break through existing barriers and explore uncharted territories.

Second comes the concept of 'creativity in the arts'! For artists, writers, musicians and performers, imagination is the lifeblood of their work. It allows them to create unique, thought-provoking, and emotionally resonant pieces of art that can captivate their audiences and stand the test of time.

Visionary leadership is the third point on our list. For someone who aspires to be a successful leader, possessing a strong sense of vision and purpose is very important. This capability often helps in inspiring and motivating their teams. Imagination also helps leaders envision a better future and strategize how to bring that vision to life.

Fourthly, adaptability and resilience are there. In an ever-changing world, adaptability is a valuable trait. Imagination enables individuals and organizations to envision new possibilities and pivot when faced with challenges or disruptions. Fifth would be personal growth and wellbeing! Cultivating imagination power enhances personal growth and well-being. It allows individuals to dream big, set ambitious goals and find fulfillment in pursuing their passions.

Sixth and last on the list is effective communication! Whether you're a public speaker, a marketer, or a teacher, the ability to convey ideas in an engaging and relatable manner relies on imagination. It helps you craft compelling narratives and connect with your audience on a deeper level.

Now that we've established the importance of imagination, let's explore concrete strategies to cultivate and harness this powerful mental faculty for success. First thing first – you can cultivate curiosity. As I have mentioned before also, curiosity is the precursor to imagination. It drives you to explore, question and seek new experiences. To cultivate your imagination, you can begin by fostering a curious mindset by learning to ask yourself questions like 'what if?' and 'why not?', thereby challenging the status quo.

Cultivating curiosity also becomes easier by exploring diverse interests and embracing uncertainty. To accomplish this and expose yourself to new ideas and perspectives, you can pursue a wide range of interests and hobbies like reading, painting and writing. Also try to embrace the ambiguity and see it as an opportunity for discovery rather than a barrier.

You can also practice immersive reading. Reading is a gateway to different worlds and perspectives. It fuels your imagination by exposing you to diverse stories, ideas and viewpoints. While developing the habit of reading, most people make the mistake of getting entangled in limited subjects, so remember to read across different genres.

I simply mean that you must not limit yourself to one type of literature or non-fiction. Rather, try to explore different subjects like fiction, history, science and philosophy to develop a well-rounded approach from the beginning. Engage in discussions and discuss what you read with others to gain new insights and interpretations. You can also keep a reading journal to record your thoughts, reflections and favorite passages in order to deepen your connection with what you read. Referring to these journals in the future can help inspire you from time to time.

Practicing mindfulness and meditation is another great method as they can help calm the mind, reduce mental clutter, and create a receptive space for imagination to flourish. Regular practice can enhance your inner ability to focus and concentrate, which is certainly crucial for deep thinking and creativity.

Meditation is also extremely powerful to increase self-awareness and help you understand your thought patterns and mental blocks. The practice of getting linked to your inner self is one of the first few steps to cultivate a sense of presence that allows you to fully engage with your imaginative processes.

Many people also like to embrace solitude to develop their imagination skills. Solitude provides the mental space necessary for imagination to thrive. It works like magic for boosting your self-reflection, brainstorming and creative thinking abilities. The results are evident in the works of uncountable poets, painters and other artists.

To benefit from solitude, you can carve out intentional alone time by scheduling periods of solitude in your daily or weekly routine. When you get into this productive me-time phase, make sure that you are disconnected from all the possible distractions by turning off your digital devices and hanging a 'do not disturb' sign on the room knob.

Another tried-and-tested approach is to surround yourself with diverse perspectives and ideas, and stimulate your own imagination. To cultivate relationships with people from different backgrounds, cultures and professions, you can attend and participate in various events, gatherings and conferences where you can learn from a variety of experts and thought leaders.

After building a network of such diverse individuals, you need to engage in constructive discussions and debates with them. This will help you garner others' ideas and opinions on different subjects, even if you don't always agree with them. You can 'agree to disagree', but it will surely be a learning experience.

Experts also advise to keep an idea journal that can serve as a dedicated space for capturing your thoughts, ideas and observations. It will be a valuable resource for nurturing your imagination, so make it a point to carry a small notebook wherever you go, so that no precious and imaginative thought is missed.

You can also use a digital note-taking app to record ideas as they come to you. Use your journal to document your most vivid dreams, inspirations from nature, and everyday observations. By reviewing these thought-provoking notes regularly, you can identify certain valuable patterns and connections in your 'train of thoughts'.

Actively engaging in creative pursuits can also exercise and strengthen your imaginative faculties. Some of the most creative activities that you can consider are writing, drawing, painting, music, dance, and crafting DIY projects. All these activities have their own perks that can help you build a better connection with your power to imagine.

For instance, writing (be it fiction, poetry or journaling) allows you to explore your thoughts and emotions while creating imaginative worlds. Visual arts like drawing and painting provide a medium for translating your imagination into tangible forms, whereas other art forms like music and dance offer opportunities to express emotions and ideas through movement and sound. However, hands-on activities like DIY projects stimulate creativity by appealing to your problem-solving and innovation skills.

Fear of failure can stifle imagination. Embrace the idea that mistakes and setbacks are part of the creative process. So, don't be afraid to take risks, and experiment with new ideas and approaches, even if they seem to be more inclined towards failure. In fact, if you go by my word, try to view failures as learning opportunities by analyzing what went wrong, adjusting your approach, and moving forward with a fresh perspective.

This will help you cultivate resilience and develop the ability to bounce back from setbacks with determination and a growth-inducing mindset.

Imagination is known to flourish better in a collaborative environment where ideas can be freely exchanged and built upon. To seek out opportunities for such constructive collaboration, you can join collaborative brainstorming sessions that can lead to the generation of innovative ideas and solutions.

You can also volunteer and participate with others in group projects to expose yourself to diverse perspectives and spark your creative thinking. In case this feels like a lot of work, you can create your own creative community (online or in-person) that is dedicated to creative pursuits, so that you can use that platform to draw support and inspiration.

Daydreaming may seem counterproductive, but it is indeed a natural way for your mind to wander and explore imaginative scenarios. Even experienced child psychologists suggest new parents to leave their children to get bored for a while every now and then. This activity helps them develop creativity to explore beyond toys, and serves as a stepping stone to build creativity in their hearts.

To harness this hidden power, you can allocate a designated time for daydreaming by allowing yourself short breaks during the day to let your mind wander freely. Think about the challenges or creative projects during these moments of mental freedom, and soon before you realize it, 'daydreaming' will emerge as a problem-solving tool for you.

Nature has also been a timeless source of inspiration for artists, scientists and thinkers. I truly believe that time well spent in nature has tremendous power to help heal your inner self and make you feel refreshed and rejuvenated to thrive in the competitive world that you live in. Therefore, I strongly recommend spending time in natural settings to observe the beauty and complexity of the natural world.

You can use this time to connect with the tranquility of nature to clear your mind and allow imaginative thoughts to emerge effortlessly. While at it, do not forget to find metaphors and analogies in nature that relate to your creative or problem-solving endeavors. This is an easy yet rewarding approach that you simply need to try.

Do not worry; I have many tricks up my sleeve, and the next one is learning from the masters. Studying the works and lives of creative and imaginative individuals can offer valuable insights. That is one of the key reasons why I started off the book with inspiring quotes of some influential people in their respective fields.

You should read biographies, autobiographies and interviews of renowned artists, scientists and innovators. But do not just read these masterpieces out loud like a script. Read them with the aim to understand their creative processes, sources of inspiration, and how they overcame their unique challenges in life.

You need to remember that learning is a constant process. Acquiring new knowledge and skills broadens your mental toolkit, providing more resources for your imagination. To approach continuous learning for life, you need to stay curious and committed to expanding your knowledge all the time.

You can take certain courses and training workshops to acquaint yourself with new concepts and perspectives. In case you are not interested in formal education, you can also indulge in cross-disciplinary learning to explore areas outside your primary field of interest. This can also help you make unexpected connections and trigger imaginative insights.

Getting a vision board is also a great idea to move forward. A vision board is a visual representation of your goals, aspirations and desires. It serves as a constant reminder of your dreams and can fuel your imagination. To shape a promising vision board, you can gather images, quotes and symbols that represent your goals and aspirations.

After setting this up, all you need to do is arrange them on a board or digital platform in a way that resonates with you, your personality and your life goals. Remember to place your vision board where you can see it daily to reinforce your commitment to your dreams, because as they say, visibility helps sell.

Whichever path you choose to walk on, remember to practice empathy. It is a powerful tool for imagination as it allows you to step into someone else's shoes and understand their experiences and emotions. To enhance your empathy, you need to start by paying close attention and listening to others actively in order to understand their perspectives.

Then there are thoughtful parts of literature that you can read, or movies that you can watch to explore diverse characters and viewpoints. Engaging in volunteer work or community service also works wonders to connect with people from different backgrounds and develop empathy towards them.

Other than being a mandatory tool that leads to excel in the modern world, technology can also serve as a valuable ally in enhancing your imagination. Although we use several digital tools and platforms in our daily lives, including technologies like virtual reality (VR) and augmented reality (AR) can immerse you in imaginative and interactive experiences.

If the idea of exploring new creative mediums and experimenting with digital tools excites you, you can make use of some digital art and design software to bring your imaginative ideas to life. There are also several online creative communities that allow you to connect with like-minded individuals and share your work for feedback and inspiration.

Just as you set goals for your career, health and personal life, you need to set specific goals for nurturing your imagination too. For starters, setting small goals can help; for instance, defining what success looks like for your imaginative endeavors, and breaking down your goals into smaller, achievable steps. Do not stop at setting goals, but also maintain a regular assessment of your progress and adjust your approach as needed.

Imagination is not always a linear process, and creative breakthroughs may take time. You can cultivate patience and embrace the journey of nurturing your imagination by avoiding to rush the creative process and allowing the ideas to develop and evolve naturally. As I have already mentioned earlier, you need to practice mindfulness to stay present and appreciate each step of the creative journey. Eventually, you need to recognize that not every idea will lead to immediate success, but each one will contribute to your growth.

Regular reflection on your imaginative endeavors is crucial for growth. So, take time to review your creative projects and assess what worked and what didn't. Also identify patterns in your creative process and find ways to refine and improve it. This way, you can celebrate your successes and acknowledge your progress, no matter how small.

See if you can share your imaginative work with others, as it can be a powerful motivator and a source of feedback and inspiration. To reap the benefits of this process, you can display your creative projects in a portfolio, gallery or online platform to seek feedback from peers, mentors or experts in your field. You can also mentor or teach others to share your knowledge and inspire their imagination.

Self-doubt can be a significant barrier in the path of unleashing your imagination. To overcome this roadblock, it is best to cultivate self-compassion by treating yourself with kindness and understanding, especially when facing creative challenges. Practicing positive self-talk is another great strategy to replace negative thoughts with affirmations that boost your confidence. For unparalleled encouragement and guidance, you have to surround yourself with a supportive network of friends and mentors.

Maintain a growth-oriented mindset that can fill your heart with the belief that abilities and intelligence can be developed through effort and learning. So, embrace a growth mindset at all times to embrace challenges as opportunities for growth and learning. This will also help you view your failures as little speed bumps on the path to mastering a field and staying open to new ideas and perspectives, thereby continually expanding your imaginative horizons.

As I have already said – imagination doesn't always require grand moments of inspiration; it can thrive in the everyday life too. Train yourself to find inspiration in everyday objects and scenes by observing the details and considering their potential in imaginative endeavors. Remember that even the most ordinary people have a unique narrative that can spark your creativity. So, there is no shortcut to exploring, reimagining and transforming the mundane routines and familiar rituals that are scattered around you.

Allow me to quote Bill Gates for better understanding - "We all need people who will give us feedback. That's how we improve." Well, I couldn't agree more! Feedback is a valuable resource for refining your imaginative work. So, remember to actively seek feedback from your mentors, peers or experts in your field and use it as a tool for growth. Be open to constructive criticism and be willing to iterate on your ideas and projects.

When aspiring business owners come to me for the best piece of advice, I always start by saying that they should always maintain a healthy worklife balance. Overall, balance is essential for sustaining creativity and imagination. Ensure that you maintain a healthy work-life balance, prioritize self-care, and recharge your creative energy regularly. Soon enough, you will notice that imagination thrives when your mind is rested and inspired by diverse experiences.

The creative process can be challenging and filled with setbacks. By cultivating resilience, you will feel empowered to embrace failure as a learning opportunity and develop coping strategies for handling rejection and criticism. So, if you want to persist in the face of obstacles, setbacks and self-doubt, cultivating resilience is an inseparable part of the process.

All work and no play can indeed make Jack a dull boy! Playfulness is a natural state of imagination. Allow yourself to engage in playful activities that encourage imagination. For instance, you can play board games, engage in creative hobbies, or explore outdoor activities. This will help encourage your inner child to come out and enjoy the freedom of unstructured play, which brings us to the next inter-related point.

Children are often the epitome of imagination, unrestricted by societal norms and practical constraints. That is probably the biggest reason why their drawing books are filled with wonders that cannot be easily created in other phases of our lives. Well, wouldn't you agree? These little masters can teach you a lot about imagination.

You can reconnect with your inner child by pulling out an old photo album and recalling your childhood memories and interests. You can also engage in childlike wonder and curiosity by encouraging yourself to ask the all-time-hit "what if?" question, and exploring the following imaginative scenarios without judgment.

Challenge yourself regularly to push the boundaries of your imagination. To do so, you can create exercises or prompts that encourage you to think creatively, solve problems in novel ways, or envision alternative scenarios. This will really help you in challenging your imagination to expand and evolve continually.

Finally, celebrate your imaginative achievements, no matter how small or large they may be. Acknowledge your creative efforts and the impact they have on your personal and professional growth. Celebrating your creativity reinforces its value and motivates you to continue nurturing your imagination.

Cultivating imagination power for success is an ongoing journey that requires dedication, curiosity and a willingness to explore the depths of your creative mind. By following the strategies outlined in this comprehensive guide, you can unlock your imaginative potential and harness it to achieve success in your chosen field, whether it's in business, arts, science, or any other endeavor.

Remember that imagination is a limitless resource waiting to be tapped, and the more you nurture it, the more it will propel you towards a future filled with innovation, creativity, and personal fulfillment. So, embark on this imaginative journey with an open heart and an open mind, and let your imagination light the path to your success.

Imagination is not merely reserved for the realm of artistry and creativity; it is the cornerstone of progress and achievement. It's the ability to see possibilities beyond the surface level and envision a future that transcends your current circumstances. Imagination helps you believe that your goals are attainable, no matter how audacious they might seem.

Even after I have laid down a detailed path for you to cultivate your imagination power as the first step to learn how to write down your success goals meticulously, there will be times when you just do not feel it. On days when you want to but cannot find the will to imagine, here are some tried-and-tested affirmations for you to say out loud:

- "My imagination is the canvas on which I paint my dreams."
- "I embrace my creative vision and use it to shape a better future."
- "I trust in the power of my imagination to guide me toward success." - "Every challenge I encounter is an opportunity for my imagination to shine."
- "I nurture my imagination, knowing that it's the wellspring of innovation."

While imagination is the spark, written goals are the blueprint that translates your dreams into concrete actions. A goal that is articulated in writing gains clarity, specificity and intention. It moves from the abstract realm of ideas into the tangible world of possibilities. The act of writing down your goals sets an intention in motion, signaling to yourself and the universe that you are committed to realizing your aspirations.

Written goals are a powerful tool that can help you achieve your dreams and aspirations. When you take the time to write down your goals, you make them more concrete and realizable. You also give yourself a roadmap to follow, and a way to track your progress over time. There are many benefits to writing down your goals, including clarity, focus, motivation and accountability. Writing down your goals forces you to clarify what you want to achieve. This process of self-reflection can help you to identify your true priorities and motivations.

Having written goals gives you something to focus on. It helps you to stay on track and avoid distractions. Seeing your goals written down can motivate you to take action and make progress. You will certainly feel more accountable to yourself and others, who are a part of those goals. And the list does not end there – when you know that you have written down your goals and shared them with others, you are more likely to stick with them.

When writing your goals, it is important to make them specific, measurable, achievable, relevant and time-bound. This is known as the SMART goal-setting framework. Let me explain what each of these terms implies in detail! By 'specific', I clearly mean that your goals should be specific and clearly defined. For example, instead of saying "I want to be in better shape", say "I want to lose 10 pounds in 3 months".

You must ensure that your goals are measurable, so that you can track your progress and celebrate your successes. For example, instead of saying "I want to improve my public speaking skills", say "I want to be able to give a 5-minute presentation to a group of 20 people without feeling nervous". Coming back to the SMART technique, setting goals that are far from being achievable is only going to make you feel discouraged and give up. However, if your goals are too easy, you will not be motivated to achieve them. Thus, your goals should be achievable but challenging.

Your goals should be relevant to your overall values and priorities. For example, if you are not interested in public speaking, then setting a goal to improve your public speaking skills is not likely to be relevant to you. Do not forget to double-check that all these goals have a specific deadline. This will help you to stay on track and make progress. For example, instead of saying "I want to learn a new language", say "I want to be able to have a basic conversation in Spanish by the end of the year".

Once you have written down your goals, it is important to review them regularly and make sure that you are still on track. You can review your goals at least once a month to make sure that you are still on track. If you are not making progress towards a goal, adjust your plan of action or set a new deadline. You can also use your written goals to create a plan of action for how you will achieve them. A tried-and-tested way to do this is breaking them down into smaller, more manageable steps. This will make them seem less daunting and more achievable.

Tracking your progress is a great way to stay on track. You can keep a journal or use a goal-tracking app to track your progress. As you achieve your goals, be sure to celebrate your successes. This will help you to keep feeling motivated and moving forward. I cannot stress enough on the fact that written goals are a powerful tool that can help you achieve your dreams and aspirations. If you are serious about achieving your goals, I encourage you to take some time today to write them down.

1.10 Positive Affirmations for Crafting Written Goals
On that note, here are some more positive affirmations to help you craft written goals:
-         "I write my goals with purpose, and they become the foundation of my success."
-         "The ink of my written goals propels me forward with unwavering determination."
-         "With each written goal, I pave the way for my dreams to materialize." - "My goals are my guideposts, leading me steadily toward the life I desire."
-         "I transform my thoughts into written goals, and these goals shape my destiny."

Here's a quick exercise to help you test the power of knowledge that you have gained through chapter one! Find a quiet space where you can reflect and tap into your imagination. Close your eyes and envision the life you want to create for yourself. Imagine yourself achieving your biggest dreams and aspirations.

Feel the emotions, visualize the details, and immerse yourself in this vision. Open your eyes and write down these imaginative visions as concrete written goals. Craft positive affirmations that align with your imagination and written goals. Commit to reviewing your written goals and affirmations daily, allowing them to fuel your motivation and guide your actions.

By combining the force of your imagination with the structure of written goals, you embark on a transformative journey toward success in every area of your life. Remember, your imagination knows no limits, and your written goals give it the direction it needs to manifest your desires into reality.

Chapter 2: Empowering Words and Purposeful Goals

To begin this chapter, I will not be able to find a better quote than - "Your words shape your reality. Choose them wisely in your goals, and witness the transformation they bring."

Language has an astounding impact on a human's mindset! In both tangible and intangible forms, language has the power to affect the outcomes at the receiver's end. Even if you are talking to your own self (let's say practicing your daily affirmations) or reading something written by you before, the words that you hear and/or read can make a whole lot of difference.

You must have often heard others saying "it's not about what you said; it's about how you said it". Saying or writing the most powerful message in ordinary words will have less impact on the receiver's psyche as compared to an ordinary message written or said in empowering words. The same rule goes for your written goals! It is very important to use powerful words and language to inspire you to move towards your written goal with a heart full of passion and determination.

In the realm of personal development and achieving success, the influence of words cannot be underestimated. Words hold the power to shape our thoughts, beliefs and actions. They can propel us toward greatness or hold us back in a cycle of self-doubt. When you combine the force of empowering words with purposeful goal setting, you pave the way for an extraordinary transformation that touches every facet of your life.

Therefore, this chapter is aimed at providing step-by-step guidance to formulate purposeful, empowering written goals because your words shape your reality. You have to choose them wisely in your goals to witness the transformation that they bring. Let's start by learning about empowering words.

Empowering words are words that make people feel good about themselves and their abilities. They are words that encourage people to take action and achieve their goals. Some of the most common yet most empowering words that I often encourage others to use are Capability,

Confidence, Determination, Intelligence, Resilience, Strength and Worthiness.

When we use empowering words in our writing, we are sending a message to our readers that they are capable and worthy of success. In simpler words, we are helping them to build their self-esteem and confidence. Words are powerful. They can inspire, motivate, uplift and educate. They can also hurt, discourage and tear down.

When we write, we have the power to choose our words carefully. We can choose words that empower our readers and help them to feel their best. Or, we can choose words that disempower them and make them feel small and insignificant. The choice is ours! Who knew words can do that, right?
Empowering words are those that ignite a sense of positivity, strength and possibility within us. They have the potential to alter our perception of challenges, turning them into stepping stones on our journey to success. When you infuse your written goals with empowering words, you not only create a roadmap for achievement but also cultivate a mindset that thrives on resilience and innovation.

By using empowering words in your writing, you simply make people feel good about themselves and their abilities, they are more likely to take action and achieve their goals. Such words will build their self-esteem and confidence. When people are constantly told that they are capable, intelligent and worthy, they start to believe it. This helps create a positive and supportive community by creating a space where people feel valued and respected.

You know the drill now! Let's read the following positive affirmations out loud to feel empowered:
-        "I am the architect of my destiny, crafting success with every word I use."
-        "Every word I speak shapes my reality, and I choose to manifest greatness."
-        "I am worthy of all the success and happiness that comes my way." - "With empowering words, I breathe life into my goals and watch them flourish."

Throughout history, influential individuals have harnessed the power of words to inspire change, unite nations, and fuel progress. Leaders, thinkers and visionaries have understood that their words have the ability to transcend time, and shape the course of human history. By carefully selecting words that resonate with their goals, they have been able to rally support, create movements, and achieve remarkable feats.

Empowering words are often used in historical writings to inspire readers and to teach them about the struggles and triumphs of people in the past. For example, in his famous "I Have a Dream" speech, Martin Luther King Jr. used empowering words to call for racial equality and justice. He said, "I have a dream that one day this nation will rise up and live out the true meaning of its creed: 'We hold these truths to be self-evident, that all men are created equal.'" King's words inspired millions of people to fight for civil rights, and they continue to inspire people today.

Another example of the use of empowering words in historical writings is the Declaration of Independence. This document, which was written by Thomas Jefferson in 1776, declared the independence of the United States from Great Britain. Jefferson used empowering words to justify the colonists' decision to rebel, and to inspire them to fight for their freedom.

He wrote, "We hold these truths to be self-evident, that all men are created equal, that they are endowed by their Creator with certain unalienable Rights, that among these are Life, Liberty and the pursuit of Happiness." The Declaration of Independence is one of the most important historical documents in the world, and it has inspired people all over the globe to fight for their freedom.

Empowering words can also be used in historical writings to teach readers about the struggles of people who have been oppressed or marginalized to cultivate empathy in their hearts. For example, in his book "The Autobiography of Malcolm X," Malcolm X wrote about his experiences growing up black in America.

He also wrote about the history of racism in the United States, and about the importance of black pride and self-determination. Let's take a sentence from his book for perusal - "The future belongs to those who believe in the beauty of their dreams." This quote is empowering because it shows that it is possible to overcome even the most difficult challenges if you believe in your ability to achieve your goals.

Let's discuss another example – the book "The Diary of a Young Girl" by Anne Frank. Anne was a Jewish teenager who lived in hiding during the Holocaust. In her diary, she wrote about her experiences living in fear and uncertainty. She also wrote about her hopes and dreams for the future. Anne's words are empowering because they show that it is possible to maintain hope and dignity even in the most difficult of circumstances. They also teach readers about the importance of standing up for what is right, even when it is difficult.

Earning a name in the business world is not as easy as it may sound! As an accomplished entrepreneur known for his strategic thinking and business acumen, I can certainly testify as someone who has harnessed the influence of empowering words. In my journey to success, I choose words that reflect innovation, collaboration and growth. By integrating these words into my written goals, not only do I manage to define my objectives clearly, but also imbue them with a sense of purpose, so that they can guide my actions in the future.

There had been times when I needed to create an unforgettable impact on my audience or readers through the use of powerful words and language. Be it keeping my team members motivated to meet a critical deadline, taking a leap of faith for business expansion when the others were advising me to pack up, or encouraging my own self at desperate times to be focused and confident – a part of everything significantly depended on my ability to use language to my favor.

Fortunately, my success is a living proof that I managed to do well. I founded many businesses, some of which were aimed at public welfare in the best way possible. In fact, this is one of the biggest reasons that urged me to pen down this book and share my insights with all of you using the miracle of 'empowering words'.

While empowering words are a cornerstone, they gain their true potency when combined with purposeful goal setting. Purposeful goals are those that are well-defined, specific and properly aligned with your aspirations and values. When you articulate your goals using empowering language, you create a synergy that drives motivation, amplifies focus, and fosters a deep sense of commitment.

Being a powerful tool for motivation, personal growth and success, the process of setting purposeful goals does not only allow you to strive to achieve something for the sake of it. In fact, it facilitates setting goals that will help you live your best life and make a difference in the world as a contributing member of the society.

There are many benefits to purposeful goal setting, including increased motivation, improved performance, greater sense of achievement and a wholesome life to look forward to. When you have goals that you are passionate about, you are more likely to be motivated to work hard and achieve them. These clear and specific goals better equip you to focus your energy and efforts in the right direction. This can lead to improved performance in all areas of your life.

Not only achieving these goals but even working towards achieving them fills you with a sense of accomplishment and satisfaction. This can boost your self-confidence and self-esteem, and you will start living your life in alignment with your values and purpose. Needless to say, your life will become more happy and wholesome, something to rise up for every morning packed with new hopes and aspirations to conquer another challenge.

To start setting purposeful goals, you need to identify your values and purpose. Ask yourself these questions – What is important to you in life? What do you want to achieve? What impact do you want to have on the world? Once you have a clear understanding of your values and purpose, you can start to set goals that are aligned with them.

Here are some noteworthy examples of purposeful goals infused with the power of empowering words:
-        "I will elevate my leadership skills through continuous learning, guiding my team to unprecedented success."
-        "I am resolute in transforming obstacles into opportunities, propelling my business to new heights."

27

-        "I will foster a culture of positivity and growth, nurturing an environment that breeds success."

My journey involves setting purposeful goals that encapsulate my aspirations and aligning them with empowering words. Rather than writing down immeasurable goals using plain words, I strive hard for choosing words that are impactful and help me create measurable objectives. For instance, my set goals look like "Lead my team with innovative strategies, resulting in a 25% increase in productivity within the next quarter."

For beginners trying their luck with setting realistic yet encouraging goals for themselves in the right manner, I would like to take the abovementioned goal as a reference. You can notice that by weaving empowering words like 'innovative' and 'lead' into this goal, I have managed to outline a clear path while infusing it with inspiration.

Now it is time to test your learning! To acknowledge your take-homes from this chapter, start by reviewing your existing goals and affirmations. Identify empowering words that resonate with your personal values and aspirations, and try to reword your goals, integrating these empowering words to add depth and clarity.

While at it, ensure that your goals are specific, measurable, achievable, relevant and time-bound (SMART). Do not forget to commit to daily positive affirmations that align with your empowering words and goals, and you can soon master the art of setting goals using the most impactful words that can literally cause a stir.

By weaving the influence of empowering words into your written goals, you bridge the gap between imagination and reality. Following the footsteps of notable individuals, like Jason Cardiff (yes, that's me), you'll recognize how the right words, strategically integrated into your goals, become a catalyst for personal growth and success in all areas of your life.

Chapter 3: Innovation and Goal Execution

Innovation thrives on intention. Your written goals fuel the innovation needed to excel in every aspect of life. This chapter is designed to unpack the role of innovation in personal and professional success by offering practical strategies to take action and execute your goals effectively.

In the pursuit of success, innovation is the driving force that propels you beyond the ordinary. By embracing the spirit of innovation with the deliberate guidance of written goals, you create a dynamic synergy that not only fuels your journey but also cultivates a mindset of continuous growth. This chapter delves into the profound impact of innovation in goal execution, drawing inspiration from the world of professional athletes who exemplify the transformative power of innovation in sports.

Innovation is more than a buzzword; it's a mindset that challenges the status quo and seeks creative solutions. Innovation allows you to explore uncharted territories, discover new perspectives, and uncover novel approaches to achieving your goals. When you mix your written goals with the spirit of innovation, you pave the way for groundbreaking strategies and unexpected breakthroughs.

Moreover, innovation is the process of creating new ideas or solutions that have a positive impact on the world. It is an essential driver of economic growth and social progress. Innovation can take many forms, from new products and services to new ways of doing things. The dynamics of innovation are complex and constantly evolving. However, there are some key factors that contribute to successful innovation. These include manifesting a culture of innovation, investing in research and development, effective collaboration, and studying market demand.

Setting a system to value and support new ideas, the culture of innovation encourages creativity, risk-taking and failure. It also lays down a roadmap to invest in research and development that is essential for innovation. Judicious R&D investment can go a long way in developing new knowledge and technologies that can be used to create new products and services.

To pave way for innovation, striking collaboration between different stakeholders (such as businesses, universities and governments) is an inevitable part of the process. Collaboration can help break down silos, and share ideas and resources. Another sure-shot way to drive innovation is studying market demand for new products and services to understand about the type of businesses that are more likely to invest in innovation.

Now let's consider an example to understand the dynamics of innovation in a better way. In the early 1970s, the development of the microprocessor revolutionized the electronics industry. The microprocessor is a small integrated circuit that contains the central processing unit (CPU) of a computer. It is the brain of all modern computers and electronic devices, and its development was driven by a number of factors, including all the parameters that were listed above.

The semiconductor industry in the early 1970s was characterized by a culture of innovation. Companies such as Intel and Texas Instruments were constantly investing in R&D to develop new and innovative products. Intel invested heavily in R&D to develop the first microprocessor, the Intel 4004. The Intel 4004 was released in 1971 and was the first commercial microprocessor.

The development of the microprocessor required collaboration between different stakeholders, such as Intel, Texas Instruments, and computer manufacturers. Intel collaborated with Texas Instruments to develop the first microprocessor standard, the Intel 8086. There was a growing demand for new and innovative electronic devices in the early

1970s. This demand was driven by the rise of personal computers and other electronic devices.

The development of the microprocessor had a profound impact on the electronics industry. It led to the development of new and innovative products, such as personal computers, mobile phones, and digital cameras. It also made electronic devices more affordable and accessible to a wider range of people.

The dynamics of innovation can be seen in other industries as well. For example, the development of the internet revolutionized the telecommunications industry. The development of the smartphone revolutionized the mobile phone industry, and the development of artificial intelligence (AI) is revolutionizing many industries, including healthcare, finance and manufacturing.

The dynamics of innovation are important for a number of reasons. First, innovation drives economic growth. New products and services create new jobs and industries. Second, innovation improves our quality of life. New products and services can make our lives easier, healthier, and more enjoyable. Third, innovation helps us to solve some of the world's most pressing problems, such as climate change and poverty.

Let me make it simpler by giving you the reference of application of the dynamics of innovation in different industries. In the healthcare industry, innovation is leading to the development of new drugs, treatments and medical devices. For example, the development of immunotherapy has revolutionized the treatment of cancer. In the education industry, innovation is leading to the development of new teaching methods and technologies. For example, the use of online learning and artificial intelligence is helping to personalize education and make it more accessible to students around the world.

However, in the energy industry, innovation is leading to the development of new renewable energy sources and energy storage technologies. For example, the development of solar and wind power is helping to reduce our reliance on fossil fuels. The dynamics of innovation are constantly changing, but it is noteworthy that the key factors that efficiently contribute to successful innovation remain the same. Let us refer to a good athlete's approach to innovation for added clarity!

Innovation is the process of creating new or improved products, services or processes. It is essential for all industries, including sports. Professional athletes are prime examples of how innovation can elevate performance to unparalleled heights. These individuals consistently push their physical and mental boundaries, seeking innovative techniques to gain a competitive edge. Whether it's refining their training methods, adopting cutting-edge technology, or employing mental strategies, athletes understand that innovation is a crucial ingredient in achieving victory.

Innovation in sports can lead to a variety of benefits. New technologies and training methods can help athletes improve their speed, strength, endurance and other physical skills. Wearable sensors, video analysis software, and other technologies are being used to help athletes improve their performance and reduce their risk of injury. For example, the NBA uses a system called Second Spectrum to track player movements and performance data in real time. This data is used by coaches to make adjustments to their game plans and by players to identify areas where they need to improve.

New equipment and safety protocols can help to reduce the risk of injuries to athletes. For example, helmets with advanced concussion protection have helped to make sports like football and hockey safer. Innovation can make sports more accessible and enjoyable for people of all ages and abilities. For example, adaptive sports equipment such as running blades and wheelchairs allows people with disabilities to participate in sports that they might not otherwise be able to.

Innovation can also be used to enhance the sports experience for fans. For example, virtual reality and augmented reality technologies can be used to give fans a more immersive experience at sporting events. And social media platforms are being used to connect fans with each other and with their favorite teams and athletes.

New training methods are being developed to help athletes improve their performance and reduce their risk of injury. For example, interval training and cross-training have become popular ways to improve athletic fitness. And sports psychologists are helping athletes to develop mental toughness and resilience. Innovation can also help promote sportsmanship and fair play. For example, the development of instant replay technology has helped to reduce the number of disputed calls in sports.

As I've said earlier, innovation involves pushing the boundaries of what you believe is achievable, especially when you talk about the realm of written goals. It's about exploring new avenues, questioning assumptions, and embracing failure as a stepping stone toward success. With innovation by your side, you will not only be able to craft a roadmap for your journey but also open doors to uncharted territories of growth and achievement via your written goals.

Innovation is not just about developing new products and services. It can also involve finding new and better ways to do things, such as improving processes or reducing costs. Innovation is not just for large businesses. Small businesses and individuals can also innovate and succeed. After all, it is not a one-time event, but an ongoing process that requires continuous investment and effort.

In today's world, it is more important than ever to embrace innovation. By doing so, businesses and individuals can stay ahead of the competition and create a better future for themselves and others. If you are wondering about how to embrace innovation in your everyday life, let me give you some nice tips that had helped me, and I have also heard good reviews from people to whom I suggested using these tips.

First of all, you need to remember that the world is constantly changing, and new skills are always in demand. By learning new skills, you can make yourself more marketable and adaptable to change. So, be open to new ideas. Don't be afraid to try new things and challenge the status quo. The best innovations often come from thinking outside the box.

Being willing to collaborate with others is also a great way to innovate your life. Innovation is often a collaborative process. By working with others, you can benefit from their ideas and expertise. Innovation often involves taking risks, so take the fear of failure out of your heart because failure is a natural part of the learning process. By embracing innovation, we can all create a better future for ourselves and others.

Thinking about how your innovative goals should look like? Here's a sneak peek:
- 	"I will revolutionize my industry by introducing a disruptive product that addresses a critical market need."
- 	"I am committed to embracing emerging technologies to enhance efficiency and customer experience."
- 	"I will pioneer a novel approach to team collaboration, fostering a culture of innovation within my organization."

The story of innovation is one of unending evolution. By combining innovative thinking with the structured guidance of written goals, you harness the potential to achieve greatness beyond your imagination. In the same vein as professional athletes who constantly redefine what's possible, you'll find that innovation is not just a means to an end; it's a journey that transforms your perception of challenges into stepping stones to success.

Let us now practice these positive affirmations out loud to embrace innovation with open arms:
- 	"I welcome innovation as a catalyst for transformation in my pursuit of success."
- 	"I thrive on thinking beyond boundaries, finding ingenious ways to conquer challenges."
- 	"Innovation is my secret weapon, propelling me toward greatness in all endeavors."
- 	"I am an innovator, and my goals reflect my commitment to pushing boundaries."

To test your ability to embrace innovation in the process of setting your goals, here is a simple exercise to perform. Start by reviewing your written goals and affirmations. Identify areas where you can infuse innovation to amplify your goal execution, and explore new strategies, methodologies or approaches that align with your goals.

Once you are done with finding out appropriate methods to help you, write down innovative affirmations that reflect your commitment to pushing boundaries. Embrace failure as a learning opportunity and adjust your goals based on your innovative insights. By embracing innovation in your written goals, you pave the way for extraordinary achievements. Following in the footsteps of professional athletes who push their limits, you'll witness how innovation becomes the cornerstone of your journey toward excellence in every area of your life.

Chapter 4: Perseverance and Overcoming Obstacles

Challenges are stepping stones in your journey, but with written goals as your guide, you can overcome any obstacle. On that note, I have some actionable techniques up my sleeve that can help you maintain focus and perseverance in the face of adversity. So, let us start with this chapter and discuss the resilience required to navigate the setbacks and challenges that you witness in your journey.

As I just said, in the path of success, challenges and obstacles are inevitable companions. However, the true measure of your journey lies not in the absence of adversity, but in your ability to persevere and rise above it. This chapter explores the profound relationship between written goals, perseverance, and the indomitable spirit required to overcome obstacles. Drawing inspiration from the world of professional athletes, we'll delve into how they embody the essence of perseverance in the face of challenges.

Perseverance is the unwavering commitment to continue moving forward despite setbacks, failures, and hardships. It's the resilience that keeps you focused on your goals even when the path seems insurmountable. By aligning your written goals with the spirit of perseverance, you transform obstacles from roadblocks into stepping stones, propelling you closer to success.

Perseverance is not easy, but it is essential for success. Every great achievement in history has been accomplished through perseverance. Whether it is climbing Mount Everest, starting a successful business, or overcoming a personal challenge, perseverance is the key to victory. There are many different ways to cultivate the art of perseverance. Let us discuss about a few tips that work like magic!

Set clear goals and break them down into smaller steps – What do you want to achieve in life? Once you know what your goals are, you can start to develop a plan to achieve them. This will help you stay motivated and focused even when things get tough. At the same time, you need to remember that large goals can be daunting. They seem much more manageable when you break them down into smaller steps. This will help you stay on track and make progress towards your ultimate goal.

Celebrate your successes but don't be afraid to fail – It is important to celebrate your successes, no matter how small it may seem. This will help you stay motivated and keep moving forward. But failure is a natural part of the learning process. Everyone fails at some point in their lives. The important thing is to learn from your mistakes and keep moving forward.

Find a support system – Sometimes, we all need somebody to rely on. Having a support system of people who believe in you and can help you stay motivated is essential. This group could include your friends, family, or even a mentor. You cannot possibly establish a sound relationship with them instantly, so let the bond grow over a period of time and remember, every relationship is 'give and take'.

Let us brush up our understanding by wrapping our head around some exemplary people who have demonstrated the art of perseverance. Thomas Edison failed over 10,000 times before he successfully invented the light bulb. J.K. Rowling was rejected by 12 different publishers before her first Harry Potter book was accepted. Michael Jordan was cut from his high school basketball team. Last but not the least, Oprah Winfrey was fired from her first job as a news anchor.

All of these names mentioned above managed to make such a big brand name for themselves by hanging to dear life with the essence of perseverance. These are just a few examples of people who have achieved great things through perseverance. Their stories show that anything is possible if you never give up on your dreams and persevere in the face of challenges

You can go ahead and read more about their stories to understand the importance of having a 'never say no' spirit, especially when problems start tormenting your life from all directions. Life is full of challenges, and one problem will follow another. Everyone faces them at some point. But the people who persevere are the ones who come out stronger on the other side.

To master the art of perseverance, acknowledging your feelings is a basic step. You must know that it is okay to feel discouraged, frustrated, or even angry when you are facing a challenge. So, don't try to bottle up your emotions. Allow yourself to feel them, and then move on. But at the same time, you also need to focus on the positive. It can be difficult to see the positive when you are facing a challenge, but it is important to try. Look for the silver lining in every situation. Remind yourself of your strengths and accomplishments.

Moreover, you need to take care of yourself, both physically and emotionally when you are facing a challenge. Make sure that you are not neglecting your overall wellbeing by getting enough sleep, eating healthy foods, and exercising regularly. Also, make time for activities that you enjoy. These activities can be of various types, depending on your interest, like reading, cooking, or simply going out in the nature.

At all times, you need to be aware of the fact that giving up on your dreams is not an option, no matter how difficult things get. Take one step at a time, and with each step, try to fill your heart with positivity and encouragement. If you keep working towards your goals with complete dedication and perseverance, you will eventually achieve them.

Perseverance brings with it, many rewards like the ability to achieve your goals, no matter how difficult they may seem. It also helps you develop resilience and confidence, which is the ability to bounce back from setbacks. By learning to persevere, not only do you get to build your own skills, but your example can inspire others to persevere through their own challenges.

The art of perseverance is a skill that can be learned and developed. It is a skill that is essential for success in all areas of life. When you learn to persevere, you will be able to overcome any challenge and achieve your dreams.

Here is a quote from the famous author and motivational speaker Jim Rohn that I find inspiring:
"Don't be afraid to fail. It's not the end of the world, and in many ways, it's the first step toward learning something and getting better at it."

This powerful quote explains that the failure is a natural part of the learning process. Everyone fails at some point in their lives. The important thing is to learn from your mistakes and keep moving forward. If you are facing a challenge right now, don't give up. Keep persevering, and eventually you will make it to the other side of the bridge.

If you wish to know my secret for cultivating perseverance, you need to practice these positive affirmations and you will immediately feel the transformation:
-        "I am unshakable in the face of challenges, persisting with determination toward my goals."
-        "Every obstacle I encounter is an opportunity to grow stronger and wiser."
-        "I embody the spirit of perseverance, turning setbacks into comebacks."
-        "With written goals as my North Star, I navigate the storms and emerge victorious."

Professional athletes offer invaluable insights into the art of perseverance. Their journeys are rife with moments of triumph and defeat, each of which contributes to their growth and resilience. Athletes understand that setbacks are not failures; they are opportunities to reassess, recalibrate, and bounce back stronger.

Some of the most common examples of athletic resilience in action are injury recovery, overcoming defeats, and consistent training. Good athletes often have to undergo rigorous rehabilitation after injuries, demonstrating their commitment to returning to peak performance. They are designed to consider defeats as stepping stones to improvement, and use failures as fuel to refine their skills and strategies. Their relentless dedication shines through in their rigorous training routines developed to WIN.

Written goals serve as beacons that guide you through the storms of adversity. When you confront challenges, your goals provide clarity and purpose, preventing you from getting derailed. Your goals remind you of the bigger picture and the achievements that await on the other side of perseverance.

Here are some impressive examples of perseverance-aligned goals: - "I will continue refining my product, addressing feedback, and iterating until it meets the highest standards of excellence."
-        "I am committed to consistently honing my skills, dedicating time each day to deliberate practice."
-        "I will persistently expand my network and reach out to potential collaborators, knowing that building connections takes time."

Infusing your goals with perseverance makes your written goals greater than mere targets; they become an embodiment of your determination. When you align your goals with the spirit of perseverance, you equip yourself with the mental fortitude needed to face challenges head-on. Every obstacle you conquer becomes a testament to your resilience, marking your journey with stories of triumph over adversity.

Moving on to the part that you had been waiting for — try out this exercise to assess if you can intertwine the spirit of perseverance with your written goals. Begin by reflecting on the past challenges that you've overcome and the lessons they've taught you. Then, review your written goals and identify the potential obstacles that may arise.

Craft written goals that include a plan for overcoming each of the obstacle that you have highlighted, and develop some positive affirmations that can reinforce your commitment to perseverance. In the face of challenges, remind yourself of your goals and affirmations to stay focused and motivated. Easy, isn't it?

This exercise might sound plain on the surface level, but it can help you create a roadmap that leads not just to success, but also to personal growth and resilience. As athletes demonstrate on the field, with each stride of perseverance, you transform challenges into stepping stones that elevate you toward victory in every area of your life.

Chapter 5: Visualization and Manifestation

I would like to start this chapter with another powerful thought, and that is:
- "Visualize your goals, manifest your destiny. Written goals set the stage for the powerful act of manifestation."

After all that we've already covered, we need to explore the science behind visualization and its impact on goal achievement. This chapter dives deep into the art of visualization and how it intertwines with written goals to create a harmonious synergy that shapes your destiny. Herein, I'll introduce some practical exercises to enhance your visualization skills and align them with your written goals. So, let's start by learning about the power of visualization!

Visualization is a powerful mental technique that can transform your dreams and goals into reality. It's a process of creating vivid mental images of what you want to achieve, and through consistent practice, these images can manifest into your life.

Visualization has been employed by athletes, artists, entrepreneurs, and countless others to enhance performance and reach their full potential. In this section designed to explore the power of visualization, we'll delve into its history, the science behind it, and practical methods to harness this remarkable tool for personal growth and success.

Visualization, often referred to as creative visualization or mental imagery, is not a new concept. It has been a part of human culture and spirituality for centuries. Indigenous cultures, for instance, have used visualization in their healing rituals, and many forms of meditation involve vivid mental imagery.

In the early 20th century, the New Thought movement popularized the idea that thoughts have the power to shape one's reality. This movement laid the foundation for modern self-help and personal development practices that often include visualization as a core component.

One of the pivotal figures in the popularization of visualization techniques was Napoleon Hill, who wrote "Think and Grow Rich" in 1937. In his book, Hill stressed the importance of creating a clear mental image of what you desire. He argued that when you hold a vivid image of your goals in your mind, it becomes a burning desire that can propel you towards success.

The effectiveness of visualization might seem mystical or esoteric, but it is grounded in psychology and neuroscience. Several studies and research findings support the power of visualization. Here's a closer look at the science behind it:

Neuroplasticity: The brain is highly adaptable and constantly rewiring itself based on experiences and mental activities. When you vividly imagine a scenario, your brain interprets it as a real experience, strengthening neural pathways associated with the skill or outcome you're visualizing.

Reticular Activating System (RAS): Your brain has a filter called the RAS, which sorts through the immense amount of sensory information it receives. When you consistently visualize a goal, it programs your RAS to pay more attention to things related to that goal. This can help you notice opportunities and resources that you might have previously overlooked.

Reduced Anxiety and Enhanced Motivation: Visualization can reduce anxiety and stress. By mentally rehearsing challenging situations, your brain becomes more prepared to face them, and this can lower anxiety levels. Visualization also creates a sense of desire and motivation that drives you to take action. When you can see and feel the achievement of your goals, it becomes a potent source of inspiration.

Skill Improvement and Pain Management: Studies have shown that athletes who engage in mental imagery alongside physical practice often see greater improvements in their performance. This suggests that visualization can enhance one's skills and abilities. Visualization techniques are also used in managing pain. For instance, patients are taught to visualize their pain diminishing, and this can lead to real reductions in pain perception.

The process of visualization can vary depending on individual preferences and goals. To engage in effective visualization, you need to start by setting and defining your goals clearly. Whether it's achieving career success, becoming healthier, or mastering a skill, you need a specific target to visualize.

To move ahead and imagine in detail, it is best to create a relaxing environment. To do so, you can find a quiet, comfortable place to sit or lie down. Close your eyes and take deep breaths to relax your body and mind. This will help you create a mental picture of your goal. Visualize every detail – the sights, sounds, smells and feelings associated with your success. Make it as vivid and realistic as possible.

You can then engage all your senses to make your visualization more powerful. Feel the excitement, joy or satisfaction that your success brings. The more senses you involve, the more real it will feel. While at it, do not forget to practice regularly. Visualization is most effective when practiced consistently. Set aside time each day to visualize your goals, ideally once in the morning and once before sleep.

At all times, you have to maintain a positive attitude during your visualization practice sessions. Believe in your ability to achieve your goals, and nurture your inner confidence as it is a crucial component to visualize and take the inspired action successfully. Visualization is not a substitute for action. It's a tool to prepare your mind for the actions you need to take. As you visualize, consider the steps you must take to reach your goals, and then act on them.

The power of visualization is evident in various aspects of life – from sports and art to personal development and business. Here are some real-world examples of how individuals and groups have harnessed the power of visualization:

Sports Performance – Athletes often employ visualization techniques to enhance their performance. They mentally rehearse their moves, strategies and even the feeling of victory. By doing so, they improve their focus, confidence and overall performance. For instance, golfers visualize the perfect swing, runners imagine crossing the finish line first, and basketball players picture themselves sinking that game-winning shot.

Creative Arts – Artists, musicians and writers also rely on visualization. Writers, for example, often create a mental image of their story or characters before putting it into words. Visual artists visualize their artwork before they ever put brush to canvas. Musicians imagine themselves giving a stellar performance, which boosts their confidence and reduces performance anxiety.

Personal Development – In the realm of personal development, visualization techniques have been widely used to achieve various life goals. This includes improving self-confidence, reducing anxiety, achieving financial success, or creating a healthier lifestyle. When individuals consistently visualize these achievements, they are more likely to take actions that lead to the desired real change.

Business and Entrepreneurship – Entrepreneurs and business leaders harness the power of visualization to set and achieve business goals. They create a clear mental image of what they want their company to become, and this vision drives their strategic decisions and daily actions.

Successful entrepreneurs often attribute their achievements to having a clear vision and the determination to see it through.

Stress Reduction and Health – Visualization is used in the aspects of stress reduction and promoting physical and mental health too. Patients facing surgery may visualize a successful and pain-free operation, which can lead to a more positive outcome. People with chronic illnesses use visualization to manage pain and discomfort. Additionally, those practicing meditation often use visualization to reach a state of deep relaxation and mindfulness.

To make the most of visualization, you need to be equal parts consistent and positive. Remember that regular practice is very important, and so, you need to set aside dedicated time each day for visualization. Maintain a positive mindset during your practice, and focus on what you want, rather than what you don't want.

As you visualize, feel the emotions associated with your success. The stronger the emotions, the more effective the visualization. Engage all your senses to create a complete mental image of your goal, and pair your visualizations with positive affirmations related to your goals. This reinforces the message to your subconscious mind.

There is no substitute to developing belief in yourself to take action. Self-doubt can diminish the power of visualization, so have confidence in your ability to achieve your goals. Visualization is a potent tool to improve yourself and prepare your mind for action. Don't forget to take real steps toward your goals.

You will be mistaken if you take visualization as a magic wand that will transform your life overnight. There are some challenges and limitations associated with visualization, which you need to steer clear of. So, remember that you can never over-depend on visualization as relying solely on visualization without taking action is unlikely to lead to significant results. It's essential to complement visualization with concrete steps.

Another roadblock is that t he effectiveness of visualization can vary from person to person. Some individuals might find it more challenging to create vivid mental images, while others might have a natural talent for it. Visualization is a gradual process that needs patience and persistence, so you do not need to frown if you fail to see tangible results instantly.

There are always some external factors that are beyond our control to potentially hamper the achievement of your goals. In such cases, visualization can only take you ahead to a certain level. As I already said, you cannot depend on visualization entirely by ruling out any possible risks associated with its variable power.

The power of visualization lies in its ability to shape your beliefs, attitudes and actions, ultimately influencing your reality. When you consistently and vividly picture your goals, your subconscious mind takes notice, and you begin to notice opportunities and possibilities that were previously invisible.

As you embark on your journey of visualization, remember that it's not a substitute for hard work, determination and action. Rather, it's a complementary tool that can enhance your focus, motivation, and confidence as you work towards your aspirations. Whether you seek to excel in sports, arts, business or personal development, the power of visualization can be a guiding light on your path to success. So, close your eyes, visualize your dreams, and let your imagination pave the way to a brighter future.

In the pursuit of your dreams, visualization emerges as a valuable tool that bridges the gap between imagination and reality. By seamlessly integrating the practice of visualization with your written goals, you unlock the profound potential to manifest your aspirations into tangible results.

I have repeatedly stressed on the fact that harnessing the power of visualization is not a one-day endeavor. Either you are a natural, or you have to learn it the hard way by employing the required time and effort. Visualization is the art of vividly imagining yourself in a situation, experiencing it with all your senses.

When you immerse yourself in these mental scenarios, you're not just daydreaming; you're priming your mind to recognize and seize opportunities that align with your goals. Visualization ignites your subconscious mind, prompting it to guide your actions toward your desired outcomes.

To train your mental faculty to visualize for a successful and contented life, these positive affirmations can work wonders:
-        "I harness the power of my mind to visualize and manifest my goals." - "Through visualization, I bring my dreams to life and make them my reality."
-        "My thoughts and emotions are aligned with the success I envision." - "With each visualization, I am one step closer to turning my dreams into reality."

Now let us move on to manifestation! Manifestation is the process of turning thoughts and intentions into concrete experiences. When you pair the intentionality of your written goals with the vividness of visualization, you initiate a sequence of actions and decisions that steer your reality toward your envisioned outcome. Visualization helps you cultivate the belief that your goals are not just possible, but inevitable.

Let's learn how to invoke the power of visualization for successful manifestation with this simple exercise. This is something that we have already talked before but I believe that summing it up in the form of an exercise will allow you to experience this transformation first-hand. All you need to do is find a quiet space where you can relax without distractions. Close your eyes and envision your written goals as already achieved.

Engage all your senses to make the visualization as vivid as possible. Feel the emotions that success brings, allowing them to fill your being. Now open your eyes and carry the feeling of accomplishment throughout your day. Doesn't the day look sunnier than usual today? Well, as you weave the practice of visualization into your written goals, you merge intention with action, and imagination with reality.

Every moment you spend visualizing success becomes an investment in your future. Through this harmonious synergy, you not only shape your destiny but also unlock the hidden potential within you, fostering a life that transcends mere aspirations and manifests the extraordinary.

Chapter 6: Accountability and Support

Beginning another great chapter with another great thought! - "Accountability fuels progress. Written goals hold you accountable, and a supportive network propels you forward."

Accountability and support are two fundamental pillars that you need to stand tall in any sphere of life. They serve as guiding principles in goal setting, execution and achievement, providing structure, motivation and resilience throughout the journey. Considering the unparalleled importance of accountability and support in maintaining a healthy momentum required for a successful life, I wanted to highlight some key strategies that can help build a support system, and enhance your journey toward success.

In the comprehensive exploration that you are going to witness in this chapter, we will delve into the significance of these two interconnected concepts, their influence on goal attainment, and practical strategies for applying them effectively. So, let us begin this great chapter by brushing up your understanding around the role of accountability and support in the process of goal attainment.

So, what do I mean when I say 'accountability'? Accountability is the state of being responsible for one's actions, decisions and outcomes. It entails taking ownership of your commitments and acknowledging the consequences of your choices, whether positive or negative. In the context of goal attainment, accountability means holding yourself answerable for the progress and results of your efforts.

Coming next to support – it encompasses the assistance, guidance, resources and encouragement that individuals receive from various sources, such as mentors, friends, family, colleagues, or even oneself. This support can come in emotional, financial, informational or instrumental forms, and it plays a vital role in helping individuals overcome obstacles and stay on track to reach their goals.

Accountability is a foundational element in the pursuit of goals, and its importance can be viewed from several perspectives. When you hold yourself accountable for your goals, you gain clarity and focus. You clearly define what you want to achieve, the steps required to get there, and the timeline for achieving it. This structured approach eliminates distractions and keeps you on course.

The attribute of accountability reinforces your commitment to your goals. When you're accountable to yourself or others, you're more likely to stay motivated. The knowledge that you'll be answerable for your progress and outcomes is a powerful incentive to keep pushing forward without any ado.

It is important to assess whether you're on track, identify areas where you might be falling short, and make adjustments as needed. Accountability encourages the regular measurement and evaluation of your progress. This ongoing evaluation is essential for effective goal management and attainment.

By being accountable, you take responsibility for the outcomes of your efforts. Whether you succeed or face setbacks, you own the results and learn from them. This helps in personal growth and the development of problem-solving skills. Accountability also builds trust, both in yourself and among those who are involved or interested in your goals. When you consistently deliver on your commitments, you gain the trust and confidence of others, which can lead to valuable partnerships and collaborations.

Support is equally crucial for recognizing and attaining your goals. It matters a lot as a tool to overcome challenges, sustain motivation, gain knowledge and expertise, develop emotional resilience, and garner valuable feedback for improvement. Goals often involve challenges and obstacles, and support provides the necessary resources and guidance to overcome them. Whether it's seeking advice from a mentor or receiving encouragement from friends and family, support can be the key to navigating difficulties.

The journey toward achieving your goals can be long and arduous. Support systems, including those who believe in your abilities and provide encouragement, help sustain your motivation during tough times. Support also comes in the form of knowledge and expertise. Mentors, advisors or experts in your field can offer insights, advice and strategies that can significantly accelerate your progress toward your goals.

Another crucial aspect of support is emotional support that helps maintain resilience. The belief and care of friends and family can boost your emotional well-being, helping you handle the emotional ups and downs that come with pursuing challenging goals. Support systems, such as mentors or accountability partners, can offer valuable feedback and guidance. They can hold you accountable for your actions, providing constructive criticism and direction to help you stay on track.

Accountability and support are not mutually exclusive; they complement and reinforce each other in the pursuit of goals. The interplay between these two concepts is essential for many reasons like setting clear expectations. Accountability begins by setting clear expectations for your goals. Whether you're setting expectations for yourself or with a team, it's essential to establish what needs to be achieved and the responsibilities of each party involved.

Another way that both of these concepts go hand-in-hand is via accountability partners like friends, colleagues and mentors who provide the support necessary to help you achieve your goals. They not only hold you accountable but also offer guidance and motivation along the way. Accountability involves regular monitoring and evaluation of your progress. In this process, support systems play a role in providing feedback and suggestions for improvement.

When challenges or setbacks occur, support systems offer emotional resilience, helping you bounce back from disappointments. They provide a safety net to help you maintain your focus and motivation. Support can help you access the resources needed to achieve your goals, whether that's through financial support, introductions to key contacts, or access to necessary information and materials.

Now that we've established the importance of accountability and support in recognizing and attaining your goals, let's explore practical strategies for incorporating these principles into your goal-setting process. The first thing that you need to do here is defining clear, well-defined, measurable and specific goals as vague or unclear objectives make it challenging to hold yourself accountable or seek appropriate support.

Post this, you need to develop a detailed action plan that outlines the steps required to achieve your goals. This plan should include timelines, milestones and any resources needed. This clarity in your approach facilitates the accountability and support process. Thereafter, carefully select individuals or groups who can serve as your accountability partners. These could be friends, mentors, colleagues or even online communities related to your goals. Share your goals and action plan with them.

Establish regular check-in points with your accountability partners. For instance, you can set up weekly, bi-weekly, or monthly meetings to review your progress, discuss challenges, and receive feedback. To benefit fully from accountability, be transparent and honest about your progress. If you're falling behind or facing challenges, share this information with your accountability partners. They can provide guidance and solutions.

Create a support network that includes friends, family and mentors who can offer emotional support and encouragement. Share your aspirations with them and seek their motivation during challenging times. Stay open to learning and personal growth throughout your journey. Accountability partners and support networks can help you identify areas for improvement and suggest resources or opportunities for development.

Be flexible in your approach. If circumstances change, be ready to adapt and pivot your goals and action plan as needed. Accountability partners and support networks can offer insights during these times of adjustment. While external accountability is valuable, practice self-accountability too. Be responsible for your own actions and outcomes. Develop the discipline to track your progress and make necessary adjustments without external reminders.

Now let's explore how accountability and support can be applied to a real-world scenario – career advancement. This case study illustrates how these principles play a crucial role in professional development. Here's the scenario: Sarah, a mid-level manager in a corporate setting, aspires to reach the executive level within the next five years.

Sarah clearly defines her career goals, including the specific role she wants to achieve and the timeline for reaching it. She writes this down in a career development plan, and establishes a bi-weekly check-in with her mentor, a senior executive in the company. During these meetings, she shares her progress, discusses challenges, and receives feedback on her career development activities.

Sarah is open with her mentor about her progress. If she encounters obstacles or misses deadlines, she communicates this honestly, allowing her mentor to provide guidance and support. Sarah's mentor offers valuable guidance on the skills and experiences needed for an executive role. He provides recommendations for professional development opportunities, including courses, workshops and networking events.

Sarah's family and friends provide emotional support by encouraging her and acknowledging her achievements. Their belief in her abilities boosts her confidence and motivation. She takes advantage of resources provided by her company, such as leadership training programs and executive coaching. These resources help her build the skills necessary for her desired role.

Sarah actively seeks out industry events and connects with professionals in her field. These connections offer insights and support in the form of referrals and opportunities for career growth. In this case study, Sarah combines clear accountability practices with a robust support network to navigate her career advancement journey successfully. The combination of structured check-ins with her mentor, transparency in her progress, and a well-rounded support system contributes to her career growth.

Incorporating accountability and support into your goal attainment process may not always be straightforward. There can be challenges and barriers that you need to overcome. For instance, some individuals may resist being held accountable for their goals due to fear of failure or a desire to maintain flexibility in their actions. Overcoming this resistance may require a mindset shift and an understanding of the benefits of accountability.

Secondly, not everyone has immediate access to a strong support network. In such cases, it's essential to proactively seek out mentors, advisors, or support groups that align with your goals and values. Balancing self-accountability with external accountability can also be a challenge. You may need to find a middle ground that allows for individual initiative while benefiting from external checks and balances.

Fourthly, limited resources, whether financial or time, can pose a barrier to achieving your goals. Creative problem-solving and seeking out costeffective solutions can help mitigate this challenge. Long-term goals can also test your commitment. It's crucial to maintain motivation and resilience, which is where support systems play a critical role in keeping you on track.

While accountability is essential, being overly rigid can hinder your ability to adapt to changing circumstances. It's essential to balance structure with flexibility in your approach. Sharing your goals and progress with others can also evoke a fear of judgment. Therefore, you must remember that the right support network will provide constructive feedback and encouragement, not judgment.

In the journey to attain your goals, accountability and support are not mere concepts; they are powerful tools that can significantly enhance your chances of success. Accountability brings structure, commitment and measurement to your goals, ensuring that you take ownership of your actions and results. Support, on the other hand, offers the required resources, guidance and encouragement to overcome obstacles, stay motivated, and maintain emotional resilience.

The interplay between these two principles creates a dynamic and robust framework for recognizing and attaining your goals. By defining clear objectives, establishing accountability partnerships, and building strong support networks, you can navigate the challenges, adapt to changing circumstances, and ultimately achieve your aspirations.

Remember that the path to success is not always linear, and setbacks are a part of the journey. Accountability and support are there to guide you through the highs and lows, helping you stay on track and persevere. In the end, it's your commitment to your goals, coupled with the responsible and resilient pursuit of them, that will lead to the recognition and attainment of your dreams. Accountability and support will serve as your trusted companions in this remarkable journey.

You know what I always say – when in doubt, yell out positive affirmations. Here is a dose of positivity to get you started:
"Accountability empowers me to grow and improve."
"I embrace challenges as opportunities for growth."
"I hold myself accountable to my goals and aspirations."
"I am a positive force in my own life and in the lives of those around me."
"I am mindful of my actions and their impact on others."
"I am open to giving and receiving support when needed."
"I am accountable for creating a positive and nurturing environment."
"I am resilient and capable of overcoming challenges with support."

Ending the chapter with an exercise that can help you test and develop both accountability and support skills! Find a friend, colleague, or family member who is willing to participate in this exercise with you. Each of you should set a specific, achievable goal you want to work on. It could be related to personal development, work, fitness or any area of your life.

Establish a set of rules for accountability. For example, agree to check in with each other regularly, such as daily or weekly, to discuss your progress. During your check-in sessions, be accountable to each other. Share your progress, setbacks, and any challenges you've faced in working toward your goals.

As the accountability buddies, provide constructive and supportive feedback to each other. Encourage one another to stay on track and offer solutions to overcome obstacles. When either of you achieves a milestone or successfully reaches your goal, celebrate together. This could be a simple acknowledgment or a small reward.

Periodically, assess the effectiveness of the exercise. Are you holding each other accountable? Are you offering meaningful support? Make adjustments to your approach as needed. If you both have multiple goals or areas of improvement, you can switch roles as the one seeking accountability and the one providing support.

This exercise helps you practice being accountable for your own goals while also developing your ability to support and encourage someone else in their pursuits. It's a great way to strengthen these skills and achieve personal and mutual growth.

Chapter 7: Action, Time Management and Balance

No lost second ever returns. How you employ your time is one of the most important factors in determining your path to success, making time management an invincible armor in your toolkit. In this chapter, we will talk all about the value of time management, action and balance in life, which starts with this thought-provoking idea:
- "The clock ticks, but action propels. Written goals keep you on track as you master the art of time, balance and action."

Inspiring, isn't it? But why does it happen that the inspiring things that we read or hear somewhere are often lost in our everyday engagements, despite our promise from our inner self to adopt them into our lives? Well, I believe that happens because we do not know about the practical techniques for adopting those great words to maximize our productivity and make consistent progress. So, let us discuss about the synergy between goal pursuit, action, balance and effective time management in detail.

In the grand tapestry of achieving your goals, action is the vibrant thread that weaves your dreams into reality. When merged with the strategic guidance of written goals, action transforms from mere movement into purposeful steps that shape your destiny. This chapter tells you how to strike the perfect balance between action and time management, and how their synergy with written goals orchestrates your journey to success.

Dreams remain ethereal until action breathes life into them. Each action you take is a testament to your commitment, a deliberate stride that inches you closer to the fulfillment of your goals. Action translates intention into impact, turning the intangible into the tangible and signaling your determination to the universe.

It's not just about the quantity of actions but the quality – the thought, intention, and dedication behind each movement. When aligned with written goals, action becomes a deliberate, calculated force that propels you toward the realization of your aspirations, dreams and hopes.

Here are some positive affirmations to invoke the power of action into your lives:
- "I am the embodiment of action, propelling myself toward my aspirations."
- "Every step I take is a testament to my dedication to my goals."
- "With each action, I carve my path to success."
- "I am a doer, transforming my dreams into achievements through purposeful action."

The will to transform intentions into action is one of the first thing that you need to look out for within yourself. While intentions are the seeds of your goals, action is the sunlight and water that nurtures their growth. Written goals infuse purpose into your actions, ensuring that they are not random gestures, but strategic moves that contribute to your larger vision.

Every action becomes an affirmation of your commitment to success. When you are committed to turn intention into action, not only are you reacting to circumstances in a positive way, but you are also proactively shaping your reality. Your actions, fueled by the clarity and direction provided by your written goals, become tools for crafting the life you desire.

Let us understand more about goal-aligned actions with these examples:
- "I will allocate two hours each morning to work on my novel, bringing me closer to my completion goal."
- "I am determined to attend networking events twice a month to expand my professional connections."
- "I commit to dedicating thirty minutes daily to learning and skill development."

To fuse action with your written goals, you need to perfect the art of balancing them with your aspirations. Written goals can serve as your coach, guiding your movements with precision and purpose. With each action you undertake, you cement your dedication to your goals and ensure that you're making tangible progress. Your actions become a testament to your commitment, a series of intentional moves that collectively shape your narrative of success.

You can gradually learn how to empower your actions, here is a practical exercise for you to try! Start by reviewing your written goals and affirmations, and breaking each one of them down into actionable steps or tasks. Prioritize these tasks based on their significance to your goals. And then, create a weekly schedule that allots specific time slots for goal-related tasks. Evaluate your progress regularly and adjust your actions based on your goals' evolving needs.

Effective time management is an art that allows you to allocate your limited resources in a way that maximizes your progress. Just as a conductor carefully orchestrates each instrument's entrance and exit, you allocate your time to tasks that resonate with your written goals. Written goals become your sheet music, guiding your movements through the composition of your life.

By adhering to time management principles and pairing them with written goals, you create a symphony of progress, where each action is a note that contributes to the masterpiece you're crafting. Now let us move on to learning some tried-and-tested strategies for effective time management that can help you change the game!

First thing first — arrange tasks based on their alignment with your written goals. When your goals are your compass, you can navigate your schedule with clarity and intention. Dedicate specific time slots to work on tasks related to your goals. These blocks become dedicated periods where your actions are in harmony with your goals' intentions.

Create an environment that minimizes interruptions and distractions, allowing you to immerse yourself fully in your chosen actions. Regularly revisit your written goals to ensure your actions are in perfect synchronization. This practice will recalibrate your efforts and ensure that your actions remain aligned with your evolving aspirations.

Remember that time is your canvas, and your actions are the strokes. Written goals guide your hand to create a masterpiece of balance and achievement. Time is one of the most precious resource at your disposal. How you manage your time will help shape not only your achievements, but also your sense of balance and well-being.

The synergy between effective time management and written goals is a fundamental element that defines your journey toward success. Now let us move onto the next segment that will help you delve deeply into the art of time management, illustrating through examples how it can be both a key to harmonious accomplishment and a tool for restoring equilibrium.

As I said, time management is the art of allocating your hours and minutes with intention and purpose. When guided by written goals, your time management becomes more than just a schedule; it's a reflection of your aspirations and the actions required to fulfill them. Effective time management ensures that you make room for what matters most and helps you avoid the pitfalls of procrastination and aimless pursuits.

The skill of effective time management will come easier to you with everyday practice of these positive affirmations:
-        "I am the master of my time, using it wisely to create the life I desire." - "Every minute I invest in goal-aligned activities brings me closer to my dreams."
-        "With effective time management, I achieve more with less stress." - "I am in control of my schedule, ensuring a harmonious balance between work, play and rest."

Remember Sarah from the previous chapter? Let us consider her example again to understand how good time management looks like! Imagine Sarah, a professional striving for a successful career while maintaining a fulfilling personal life. Sarah's written goals guide her actions. She sets clear priorities by allocating focused blocks of time for her work tasks, including brainstorming sessions for creative projects.

She also dedicates quality time to her family, engaging in meaningful conversations and shared activities. Her time management reflects the wealth of her knowledge and values, ensuring that she dedicates time not only to career growth, but also to self-care and nurturing relationships for a well-rounded lifestyle.

Now let us see another example of poor time management. On the contrary to Sarah, consider John, who has written goals but struggles with time management. He often finds himself overwhelmed by multitasking and constantly shifting between tasks. His lack of structured time management leads to half-completed projects and missed deadlines.

His written goals remain unfulfilled as he loses sight of what truly matters amid all the chaos that comes uninvited with poor time management. His stress increases, impacting his work quality and personal life. How do you think John will feel exactly every day? With nowhere to flourish, his life will certainly look gloomy, reducing his chances at success.

Effective time management doesn't solely focus on professional accomplishments; it also nurtures balance. When you integrate time for selfcare, leisure, and meaningful connections into your schedule, you create a life that's fulfilling across all dimensions. Written goals act as a compass, ensuring that every action you take contributes to both your short-term achievements and your long-term well-being.

Moving on to the example of balanced time management, let us talk about Lena, a woman who exemplifies balanced time management. She aligns her written goals with time blocks for focused work, exercise and relaxation. By scheduling time to pursue hobbies, read and spend quality moments with loved ones, she creates harmony in her life. Written goals are her reminders to prioritize her personal growth while making strides toward her professional aspirations.

To empower your life with balanced time management, here's an exercise that you can practice! Review your written goals and assess your current time management practices. Identify areas where you can allocate more time to goal-aligned activities, and create a weekly schedule that includes time for work, self-care, relationships and hobbies. Ensure your time blocks are realistic and reflect your values and priorities. Regularly evaluate your time management and adjust based on your evolving goals.

In the dance of achievement, action is the choreography that brings your aspirations to life. By merging action with written goals, you create a symphony of purpose that resonates with progress, determination and fulfillment. As you master the art of time management and align your actions with your goals, you become the conductor of your destiny, orchestrating a life that is a testament to your intentional, purposeful and transformative actions. Just as each note contributes to a harmonious melody, each action contributes to a life that is a harmonious composition of your dreams and aspirations.